better together*

* This book is best read together, grownup and kid.

a akidsco.com

a
kids
book
about

a kids book about LIFE

by Rigler Elementary School

A Kids Book About
Editor Emma Wolf
Head of Design Rick DeLucco
Publisher Jelani Memory

DK
Senior Production Editor Jennifer Murray
Senior Production Controller Louise Minihane
Publishing Director Mark Searle

This American Edition, 2026
Published in the United States by DK Publishing,
a Division of Penguin Random House LLC
1745 Broadway, 20th Floor, New York, NY 10019

26 27 28 29 10 9 8 7 6 5 4 3 2 1
001—363864—Sep/26

First published in Great Britain in 2026 by
Dorling Kindersley Limited, 20 Vauxhall Bridge Road, London SW1V 2SA
A Penguin Random House Company

The authorised representative in the EEA is
Dorling Kindersley Verlag GmbH. Arnulfstr. 124, 80636 Munich, Germany.

A CIP catalogue record for this book is available from the British Library

ISBN 978-0-2418-3051-2

Printed and bound in China

www.dk.com

akidsco.com

MIX
Paper
FSC™ C018179

For all of the important people who have
taught us about life, and for all the kids
who may learn a thing or two from us.

And for the inventor of ice cream.

Intro
for grownups

Whether you're more *Carpe Diem* or *YOLO*, we are all trying to live our best lives. This is a practice, like yoga or meditation, which is why grownups may not think kids have the life experience to know how to do it.

As a fifth grade teacher, I promise our kids do a lot more than reading, writing, and arithmetic in a classroom community. And what may be surprising is that I learn as much from my students as they learn from me. One important thing they've taught me is how to live life in the present—they do this innately.

This book doesn't answer the philosophical question, "What is the meaning of life?", because that's for each individual to determine (or not!). This book is designed to encourage you to ride the waves of life, feel all the feelings, and enjoy the simple pleasures. Our hope is that when you pick up this book you're reminded that change is inevitable, and no matter your age or circumstances, you have the agency to live your life to the fullest.

HELL

We are the 5th graders
of Rigler Elementary.

And this is a book all about **LIFE**.

We know we’re just kids.

But we actually have
a lot to say when it comes
to this thing called **LIFE**.

IN FACT, we think one
of the most important things
you should know about life is...

LIFE IS
OF CH

FULL
ANGE.

What does that
CHANGE look like?

Well...

YOU'LL GO THROUGH PUBERTY (EVENTUALLY).
YOU'LL DEFINITELY CHANGE SCHOOLS.
YOUR BODY? YUP, THAT'S GOING TO CHANGE TOO.
YOU MIGHT END UP MOVING.
AND THINGS LIKE FRIENDSHIPS, AND EVEN YOUR PERSONALITY, WILL CHANGE TOO.

Maybe the only consistent thing about life is that it always looks

DIFFE

RENT.

Another big thing about life everyone should know is...

LIFE ISN'T PER-FECT.

SOME

SOME

TIMES,

THINGS GO WRONG.

TIMES,

THINGS ARE HARD.

Not everything goes your way.

There are times you might feel

DEPRESSED,
ANXIOUS,
STRESSED,
OR WORRIED.

Those times can be
especially tough.

SOMETIMES, you might feel lonely, or have to say goodbye to people you love.

THOSE TIMES ARE THE WORST.

LIFE ISN'T PERFECT.

And no one said it would be!

But, there's always a little bit of

BITTER and SWEET.

AND THE SUN WILL COME

UP AGAIN TOMORROW!

Life is all about

CHERISHING THE GOOD MOMENTS.

People spend a lot of time thinking about the past, or worrying about the future.

But where we really need to be is in the **PRESENT**.

What does that mean—
to enjoy what's in the present?

Here are some ways to practice
living life in the moment:

1. STOP AND THINK ABOUT WHAT'S HAPPENING RIGHT HERE, RIGHT NOW.

2. BE AWARE OF WHAT'S GOING ON AROUND YOU.

3. USE YOUR SENSES: WHAT DO YOU SEE? WHAT DO YOU HEAR? WHAT DO YOU FEEL?

4. TRY NOT TO WORRY TOO MUCH ABOUT WHAT'S GOING TO HAPPEN.

5. KNOW THAT YOU CAN'T CHANGE ANYTHING THAT HAS ALREADY HAPPENED.

LIFE IS NEVER A STRAIGHT LINE.

Bad things **DO** happen,
we're not going to lie to you.

But lots of good things happen too!

THINGS LIKE...

THE JOY OF GETTING A PET.
BEING WITH LOVED ONES.
THE SMELL OF A NEW PAIR OF SHOES.
TAKING A HOT SHOWER.
DRINKING COLD WATER.
PLAYING TAG WITH YOUR FRIENDS.
EATING YOUR FAVORITE FOOD.
CANDY!
SLEEPING IN.

HAVING SLEEPOVERS.
WELCOMING A NEW FAMILY MEMBER.
WINNING A BIG CHAMPIONSHIP GAME.
SCORING A GOAL IN SOCCER.
ACING AN ASSIGNMENT.
SHARING A NEW PIECE OF ART.
WHEN THERE'S A SEQUEL TO YOUR FAVORITE MOVIE.

There's no end to the things we can **LOVE** and **ENJOY** about life.

IN FACT, there are too many good things to count!

Think of the biggest number you know.

6,539,191,377,

866,931,503—

there are more good
things than **THAT**.

It's important to find a place in your heart to store all of those good things.

When it comes to living a good life, here are some things we want you to remember:

1. EMOTIONS, GOOD AND BAD, ARE A BIG PART OF LIFE. SO FEEL THEM ALL!

2. DON'T HOLD GRUDGES. IT HURTS YOU MORE THAN IT HURTS THEM.

3. TAKE GOOD CARE OF YOURSELF. TAKE GOOD CARE OF OTHERS.

4. LIFE CAN STILL BE GOOD, EVEN WHEN IT'S NOT PERFECT.

5. LIFE IS SHORT, SO LIVE IT WHILE YOU CAN!

And as bad as life may get,

YOU'RE STILL HERE.

Every day is a new opportunity
to live the life you want.

The life that fills you with joy.

THE LIFE YOU DESERVE!

We know we’re just kids.

But we already know
quite a bit about life!

AND HOPEFULLY, YOU CAN LEARN SOMETHING FROM US.

Know that you always belong

SOME

WHERE.

There's only

1 YOU,

and you only get

1 LIFE.

SO BE
YOUR

SELF!

(And always eat ice cream.)

Outro
for grownups

Now that you've finished this book, you may be wondering how to apply these insightful practices to your own life. Whether you're a kid or a grownup, first and foremost, go get some ice cream! But in all seriousness, try to enjoy all the pleasures of life alongside experiencing all of the pain—it's about balance, or as grownups like to say, "Everything in moderation."

If you're a grownup, we invite you to encourage the kids in your life to be mindful and explore what makes them unique, what they value, what makes their lives special, and what gets them through hard times. Model the practices in this book through your own choices and behaviors, because, as we know, actions speak volumes. Remind them that they always belong somewhere. And empower them to pay it forward and help someone else feel loved and supported on their own life journey.

About The Authors

The Rigler Elementary Class of 2025 is wise beyond their years, which is why they were qualified to write this book. They may have only been alive a decade when they authored this book, but they have had a plethora of experiences and learned myriad life lessons.

Among this group are class presidents, dancers, history buffs, kids who have lost a parent, kids who immigrated from other countries, musicians, mathematicians, foodies, wrestlers, linguists, comedians, Squishmallow parents, siblings, *futbolistas*, activists, and artists.

Above all else, they embody the Rigler Core Values of being kind, being mindful, being engaged, and being safe. Readers of all ages will benefit from their words of wisdom.

—Maestra Alana, Fifth Grade Teacher

Class Cover Gallery

Authors

Maestra Alana's Class

Andy Castillo Geronimo
Billie Whisler
Clio Giberson
Corbett Manzalji
Daniel Garcia Estrada
Elsbeth Griffin
Fabiana Pascual Sebastian
Faviola Cauich Ceh
J'den Arguello-Perez
Jhorwins Polanco Gonzalez
Kamara Blassingame
Lucy Cloud
Madeleine Salgado Bello
Malaysia Branch
Miley Ku-Castillo
Mira Summers
Ozzie Haessig
Vida Campos-Dea
Yahani Castillo-Interian
Yaritza Altamirano

Maestro Godoy's Class

Angie Ake
Melody Bracamontes
Lochlan Campbell
Amalia Cooper
Lena Heckman
Angelica Huish
Andrew Juarez
Ben Martin
Cora Obold Eshleman
Samantha Sanchez
Gael Vazquez Gallegos
Adah Davidson
Wilyer Castro